# Lucky Country

Poems

Gail Holst-Warhaft

Fomite
Burlington, VT

Copyright © 2018 Gail Holst-Warhaft
Author photo: Zoe Warhaft

All rights reserved. No part of this book may be reproduced in any form or by any means without the prior written consent of the publisher, except in the case of brief quotations used in reviews and certain other non-commercial uses permitted by copyright law.

Cover image: "By the Seine" © Michael Rubbo

ISBN-13: 978-1-944388-67-6
Library of Congress Control Number: 2018955404

Fomite
58 Peru Street
Burlington, VT 05401
www.fomitepress.com

*For Zellman, Zoe, and Simon,
and in memory of Jon Stallworthy*

# Books by Gail Holst-Warhaft

*Road to Rembetika*

*Theodorakis: Myth and Politics in Modern Greek Music*

*Dangerous Voices: Women's Laments
and Greek Literature*

*The Cue for Passion: Grief and its Political Uses*

*I Had Three Lives: Selected Poems of Mikis Theodorakis*

*The Collected Poems of Nikos Kavadias*

*Penelope's Confession*

*Losing Paradise: The Water Crisis in the
Mediterranean* (editor)

*The Fall of Athens*

# Contents

## I. Lucky Country   1

| | |
|---|---:|
| Lucky Country | 3 |
| Afghanistan, 1969 | 5 |
| Legacy | 8 |
| At the Ocean's Edge | 10 |
| On My Mother's Map | 14 |
| The Women of Her Generation | 15 |
| 'Indian Curry as Made by Col. Sankey's Black Cook' | 16 |
| When the Mail Comes | 18 |
| Flood Days | 19 |
| A Willing Heart | 20 |
| A Stray Metaphor | 21 |
| The Headmaster's Secret | 22 |
| Reading the Sky | 23 |
| Drawer by Drawer | 24 |
| My Mother's Garden | 25 |
| Touching Beethoven | 26 |
| Summer Storm | 27 |
| Looking Down on the Lucky Country | 29 |

## II. Grounded   31

| | |
|---|---:|
| Night Flight to Ithaca | 33 |
| Autumn in Ithaca | 35 |
| Weeds | 36 |

| | |
|---|---|
| Grounded | 37 |
| Jim Crows | 38 |
| Sketch for Summer | 39 |
| The Front Line | 40 |
| Winter Walk with Clouds | 41 |
| On the Bridge at Treman Gorge | 42 |
| The Lost Map | 43 |
| Near Field | 44 |
| Blowsy | 45 |
| Preserves | 46 |

**III. The Body Forgets**     47

| | |
|---|---|
| Naples | 49 |
| Bangkok Moon | 50 |
| Lisbon Revisited | 51 |
| Archaeology | 53 |
| Guardians | 54 |
| The Body Forgets | 55 |
| Pruning | 56 |

**IV. Three Poems for Jon Stallworthy (1/18/1935- 11/19/2014)**     57

| | |
|---|---|
| A Poet's Letters | 59 |
| Blenheim | 60 |
| Re-enactment | 61 |
| Acknowledgements | 65 |

# I. Lucky Country

# Lucky Country

They called it a lucky country—fortunate
to be an enormous island in the South Pacific,

a level playing-field for some
to rise like my cockney father, a boy

from the East End whose accent was enough
to place him in the old country. Among descendants

of convicts and their keepers he could become
a gentleman. Once he took me to see

the London he raised me on with stories
of pockets picked and jellied eels

that stuck to your ribs, of pease pudding,
Music Halls and Pearlies with shiny suits

and how a watch pinched back an hour
after selling would earn a boy a shilling.

*It's gone,* he said, *the East End I knew,*
as he stared at rows of cheap clothes

flapping in a damp wind, Indians
now selling jeans and drab dresses.

*There's a place I know where it still might be,*
he said and we left for Billingsgate market

where men in leather hats sold fish
and tankers unloaded a sluice of eels

into roiling troughs, where insults were traded
in rhyming slang, music to him,

familiar to me as his curses aimed
at cows, flat tires, children. Now

I saw my father at home in a place
where I was a stranger, a vanishing world.

Satisfied I'd caught the gist of his East
he stuck a cigarette to his lower lip

and whistled "Two Little Girls in Blue."
I doubted his London no more than Dickens'.

It was all child's play to us, the things
he did to stay alive before he came

to the empty land where a cockney lad
could turn himself into a gentleman.

# Afghanistan, 1969

In Kabul a gritty wind was blowing
when the British consul gave me the telegram:

FATHER DEAD. CALL MOTHER.
In Kabul muezzins called down the night.

The consul's bathroom had running water;
his walls were covered with trophies of travel.

An artistic couple—she sang, he played;
after dinner served by dark hands

came songs of Debussy, Ravel, Fauré.
My father, too, was fond of songs

and sang as a child in St Paul's Cathedral—
they combed the slums for boy sopranos

and paid them on Sunday in sticky buns.
Standing outside the Music Halls,

newspapers stuffed down his clothes for warmth
my father waited for the stars to appear

and dreamed he'd be the Silver King,
Prince of the Pearlies in Petticoat Lane.

The concert ended in faint applause—
no sound intruded from the streets of Kabul

as a servant brought coffee on a silver tray.
My father's eyes were as dark as his

and easily filled with tears as he sang.
He, too, had said yes sir, no sir

when the Marquis of Milford Haven stepped
into that newfangled motor he'd bought

whose engine defied the butler's skill
but my father could drive and take apart.

The wind still blew from the northern passes
where Indus and Oxus begin to flow

and the narrow valley of Bamian hid,
between folds of the Hindu Kush,

Buddhas as high as Shoreditch steeple
my father had climbed, once, for a dare.

In a tea-house I pass, a man dressed in white
plays with something he holds in a bag.

He answers my stare and pulls out a bird
that he throws away—it comes fluttering back.

Together they play this game of love—
the tall man and the small bird.

and I am a fearless child again
tossed in the air by strong brown hands.

## Legacy

These things are left me:
her wedding ring, snug

even on my right pinkie,
a cape of taffeta trimmed

with tassels, a wooden box,
its lid brass-rimmed.

What did she choose to carry
from Scotland to the raw shore

where a penniless girl might marry
a sex-starved settler? Thread,

needles, a darning egg,
a cape saved for the day

she stepped on the earth's underside?
A wisp of her mother's hair

knotted in intricate macramé
by a father who'd learned the art

of *memento mori*? Her face,
somber on faded glass,

gives no hint of intimacy.
Only the ring's glint

betrays the settler she outlived
and on her taffeta lap

a round-eyed child
stiff with starch and fear.

## At the Ocean's Edge

(i)

His Irish mother dead, his father lost
in drink, my grandfather learned to mold
loaves square or "high tin",
loading the oven as his sisters slept.

Polonius was his idol, his pattern
of probity: *Costly thy raiment
as thy purse can buy* –Shakespeare's
Presbyterian penny-wise prattler.

He took the pledge, sang in the choir
at St. Martin's Church, his Adam's apple
straining its noose. His sisters
beside him in their polished pew

cast eyes sideways for a raft.
His were willed not to wander,
but found themselves drawn to a hand,
a brown curl escaped from a hat.

What do men do with their wives in bed?
He closed his ears to dirty talk
on beer-soaked breath. In the fiery street
he let his horse amble, thoughts run

past the arm to the lace-fringed neck,
the lift of muslin over whalebone stays.
Enough. He checked desire with his whip,
flicked the horse to a tired trot.

(ii)

One summer's night in a dark hotel,
inexpert fingers damp with desire
obey the body's rude dictation
conquering yards of cambric, gussets

of ribboned lace prepared for this hour.
As she breathes beside him, he lies awake;
his frugal life has led him to
this lien on love in the thin dawn light.

(iii)

A traveler in chocolates now he drives
his trap through suburbs named for battles,
towns in a home he's never seen,
its empire painting continents pink.

He leaves his horse in the thin shade
of a peppercorn tree, carries
samples up scrubbed steps of a shop,
offers the Greek a peppermint cream.

Silent, they eat in the February heat,
dreaming of homes across the sea
that decades of saving could take them to,
lands with their history written in books.

(iv)

He moves into a brick bungalow,
solid enough to withstand all shocks—
war, influenza, the birth of his *one
fair daughter, and no more.*

He still stops each week
at the Greek's, listens to Ithacan dreams.
His is the land of Rabbie Burns;
one day he'd like to take her there,

the quiet wife who husbands his house.
Before he can grasp it, she falters,
leaves the custard smoking, struggles
to add a grocery bill. He remembers

mad Ophelia scattering herbs:
*They say the owl was a Baker's daughter...*
Owl-eyed, she stares at him,
his woman-turned-bird. He's adrift,

his dreams of a high land with stags
at bay and purple heather sink.
He cleans the crumbs she leaves unwiped,
watches her eyes, like his father's, fade.

He wades towards old age,
checks his watch face for some sign,
waits for tea, the evening news—
small pleasures at the ocean's edge.

## On My Mother's Map

How brave it looked in the schoolbooks,
this big and blushing continent
empty of history, stamped
like a royal seal on the sea!

On my mother's map her country
was the color of blood and corrections.
She could trace its source
to a jagged blot of red
that spread south and east
filling the outlines made
by men with pens and compass
who measured the ins and outs
of coasts from little boats.

# The Women of Her Generation

They smelled of Chanel Number Five
and seams divided their flesh-colored stockings.
When they kissed they left lipstick
on each other's cheeks and a cloud of powder.

They wore hats with spotted veils
adding a touch of imperfection to matte
peach skin. Cigarettes were lit
with gold lighters, never with matches.

They talked of nights on ocean liners;
in albums they kept faded snapshots
that showed them on deck playing quoits
with men in shorts and long white socks.

Home again safely they settled for life
with comfortable husbands, met for tea
or a hand of Gin Rummy, volunteered
for auxiliaries, thickened and bred.

When their men died they straightened
 their backs. Their hair was set in helmets
stiff with spray, and their fingers shook
as they lifted lighters to their cigarettes.

## 'Indian Curry as Made by Col. Sankey's Black Cook'

The paper turned to sepia,
and fretted from a lifetime's folding,
spotted where the butter spat
while onions fried, my mother
acquired it thanks to her aunt,
a maid in a mean house,
who sometimes slipped a teaspoon
or a cream-jug in her apron pocket.

*Curry paste can be procured
genuine, at Walker's, corner
Swanston Street and Flinder's
Lane*—a taste acquired
in Madras, still craved
by officers serving an empire
launched on the spice trade;
curry covered the sameness of
each day's stew.

The colonel brought his Indian
cook home with him.
A servant's servant, he insists
the recipe be followed carefully
*lest the secret of impregnating
the meat with the curry flavor be lost*—
a touch of pride inscribed

by another's pen on paper
pilfered by my mother's aunt
and handed down to me.

# When the Mail Comes

I remember your writing, the copperplate
they taught you before the war to end
all wars when other girls
teased you for your German name
and the headmistress couldn't bring herself
to announce the prize for Dux of the school
but handed you the calf-bound volume
when all other parents had left.

Those sloping letters on blue aerogrammes
followed me from Lisbon to Athens,
from Delhi to New York,
telling me the garden was dry
in the heatwave; Mrs Barrington died;
the funeral yesterday in scorching weather;
too much champagne and oysters at the pub;
read a novel by Carey, can't say
I really enjoyed it; have you seen
the latest Woody Allen film?

Letters sturdy as the hips I held
when you washed the dishes, my face pressed
against your corset's firm bones.

# Flood Days

Creeks were brown where I grew up,
slow most of the year, then rising
till they burst their banks. No school buses
ran on days when wooden bridges
shuddered against the weight of water.
Cows and sheep were marooned on islands.
My dad and I took wire-cutters
to let them into the neighbor's paddock.
We wore gumboots and waded together
through the shallow skirts of the flood
to rescue the Guernsey and the calf I'd weaned
with a bottle. We led them to higher ground,
my dad's cigarette hanging damp
from his lip, rain soaking our clothes,
happy doing what we did.

## A Willing Heart

For my father the bucket never fills.
A city man, he can tickle a car
into life but not coax milk
from the pretty Jersey who came with the farm.

She gives me what she refuses him,
unburdening herself freely to
a child's hands, a calf's pull
on swollen teats, a pain so sweet

she draws a breath, drool glinting
above the chaff.

# A Stray Metaphor

Running on the tow-path this morning
between the lake and the Delaware Canal,
from another age and country,
a metaphor strayed into my mind
as the wind fanned my damp shirt
and turned me into a Coolgardie safe.

Who else around here would know
about those bush refrigerators made of tin,
pierced in a pattern, painted dull green,
with a sheet of wet canvas hung round
so the scorching wind, as it blew through,
would keep butter cool for an hour or more?

Misplaced, outdated, it lingered
like a half-forgotten tune.

## The Headmaster's Secret

He ruled us with a disappointed rage,
a cravat tied under his brick-red chin.
When he died I learned of his secret life—
the affair he'd had with a woman painter

who'd married a doctor but thought herself
free to love where she pleased and chose
him. If I'd known the headmaster's secret
I'd have filled the hours from nine to four

not dreading the savage lash of his tongue
but picturing them down on the studio floor,
his face a darker shade of brick,
hers transformed by his ardent assault.

# Reading the Sky

My mother took lessons in reading the sky
from the captain of a cargo ship
carrying a load of stinking jute
around Cape Horn to the Indian Ocean.

Six weeks they sailed without a port
and when they'd studied the stars from the bridge
they'd seek true north in the cabin below.
If the ocean's roll disturbed their own

the captain would bark up a speaking-tube:
*Set your course east and hold her steady.*
*Heave to till I give the order!*
And the boatswain smiled as the engines slowed.

Tonight, beyond the lighthouse flash
on the starboard wing of a 747,
I search the sky for the Southern Cross
she pointed to on star-filled nights

when I was a child. Before she died
she talked to me as if to a friend,
laughing as she told me how
she'd once been wooed by a bearded captain.

# Drawer by Drawer

I took my mother's house apart
drawer by drawer—lavender bags
in a sea of black nylon, squares of linen
stained with lipstick, the kitchen drawer
we called "all sorts" still full of string
saved in careful coils, the screwdriver
with the mended handle, elastic bands
and keys for lost doors, refolded
wrapping-paper for next year's gifts,
a wooden egg for darning socks.

In drawers and cupboards all over the house,
packets of letters labeled with our names,
my brother's stamped with the Thai king's head
and thirty years of my life distilled
into aerogrammes, postcards, articles, snapshots
from towns I forgot I was ever in,
from cargo ships and Hungarian trains,
and an envelope marked for me read:
"Letters home, 1929—
—Burn before or after reading."

# My Mother's Garden

You taught me the names of flowers
that thrived in Melbourne gardens:
*love-in-the-mist*, this smudge
of blue; *kiss-me-quick*,
the pink with fleshy leaves;
*snap-dragon* that opened
a velvet mouth when squeezed;
*sweet Alice*, bordering
each bed. Planted by the homesick,
balsam in the colonial bush,
they eclipsed native flowers
that spoke a subaltern tongue.

Here, in Berkeley's gardens
the same flowers bloom.
They remind me you are
long gone, a trail of cats
at your heels, and your garden
with its pink camelia by the door.

## Touching Beethoven

In the dark front room of a brick bungalow
where Miss Marie lived with her mother
my fingers first touched Beethoven.

He woke, a cumbrous giant among
crystal vases and lace doilies
in a room where music was passed on

like a full cup of tea, without
spilling a drop. She gave no sign
she recognized the visitor crashing through

her house on clumps of chords and soaring
out her window. Her praise was saved
for when I left: *only a few have the gift.*

## Summer Storm

*Dreamy Pink* was the season's color
smeared across the lips' margins,
made to be eaten when we were fourteen.

I was the odd girl out
who left no stain on the lips
of glasses at the Malacoota pub.

A brunette with two blonde friends,
their dashing dads called me
*the only lady*. I wanted to be

a blonde heartbreaker. I never knew
the fathers took turns to call their lovers,
from the only public phone in town.

The mothers stayed behind at camp
beside the lagoon, lay on beach-towels,
their hair spread out to dry like haloes.

Their daughters were at the cutting edge
of life, already lost as allies,
busy conquering the local boys

who whistled as they passed. In a hammock
slung between two gum-trees
I wept alone over David Copperfield.

No-one saw the storm coming
until it swept away our tents
ripping the canvas walls away,

bending young gums in two
stirring a dangerous surf on the shore.
We gathered up the scattered wreckage

as the wind died and the sun lit
the ruffled water of the lagoon.
The holiday was coming to an end.

## Looking Down on the Lucky Country

We fly all day over desert—no wonder
the second-comers who tried to cross it
died. The colors are faded paint,
rivers snake like side-winders

then stop. The country gave itself
grudgingly to the ones who came
and stayed in the Stone Age. They knew
only one secret mattered: water

and where to find it, so they sang their way
across the land, memorizing each source,
bequeathing a map for survival from one
generation to the next, stopping to greet

members of their totem, passing on.
Near the coast browns turn green,
iron roofs wink in the sun,
highways lead to a busy city.

If the sea should rise and take a bite
out of this coast, it would all be gone,
this crust of settlement where we grew up
ignorant of the whole, thinking we knew it.

## II. Grounded

# Night Flight to Ithaca

I called you from the airport,
the plane blurred by sleet
as its pilot weighed the risk
of a night flight for three.

I remembered Vientiane,
nineteen sixty-nine,
a British pilot crimson
with drink, moustache grizzled,
turning to say, *this crate*
*might not leave the ground.*
I lay on a stretcher, carefree
with fever and felt no fear
as we bucked above the jungle.

This time I'm afraid.
I've never seen a snow-storm,
but not to miss a night with you
I bribed an ex-cop
to race me to La Guardia
*if anyone can get you there*
*it's me* he said, the door
of his limousine agape.

On the phone you say
*go buy yourself a brandy*
and lulled by liquor I board
the night flight for Ithaca

where you stand like Bogart
waiting on the wet tarmac.

## Autumn in Ithaca

I come from a leaner landscape
and learned to read its dun shades;
the only profusion of color was wattle,
yellowing the bush a month in Spring.

This autumn color seems too crude:
my daughter will know maple from oak
beech from buck-eye, scarlet from gold,
not olive from umber or how clean
the peeled Ghost Gum looks
in a paddock of tired summer grass.

## Weeds

My father took his last stand
with a spade against the stubborn weeds
of his Melbourne garden. *I feel a bit crook*
he said and died, his strenuous hindrance

soon reclaimed. Now Spring
has bulbs sprouting before their time—
crocus, periwinkle, daffodil, and weeds—
weeds we've contended all these years

with scant effect. We took sides,
you and I, helping what we planted,
guarding the cultivated—bearded iris,
orange poppies, lily-of-the-valley—

by stunting the uncouth, wanton weeds.
It's a losing battle, but we've learned the triumph
of small delays, when the greedy unkempt
holds at the edge of a space we've cleared.

## Grounded

On the way to the mailbox I see
our house is hawsered to the earth
by threads of shining twine.

The morning anger abates,
hard words softened
by a spider's tether.

# Jim Crows

Red-tailed hawk on the hemlock.
Closing in, raucous,
the black mob hectors

scenting blood. This time
I'm on the white side;
I want the hawk to win.

Pale-breasted he holds
his ground a while, a mouse
limp across his beak,

until the rabid bickering
unnerves him. He spreads, steadies
for take-off, grips his kill

and lifts over the trees
leaving a seething wake
of winners: the garden's theirs.

## Sketch for Summer

The forest's full of promise
like a young girl's face
or a sketch by Delacroix
lovelier unfinished.

An April sun mild
as milk glints on snow
daubing new grass.
So much hope's stored

in the half-formed leaves,
buds bright on branches;
a pity this will all ripen
into a sea of solemn green.

## The Front Line

Their honking fills the morning
like a blown conch shell.
The front line of fliers
battling an unseen force
of currents, gives way,
re-forms and moves north.

Looking up, I see,
among dark formations,
a short string of snow geese
on one flank, wings
tipped black. They've
stolen a ride on a ribbon
of gray Canada cousins.

I marvel at the valor of these squadrons
following an ancient imperative,
giving way, reforming
as they move relentlessly north.

## Winter Walk with Clouds

Walking on Roundtop Hill this morning,
the temperature steady at eight below,
sun and clouds stipple the slope,
charcoal on white.

Last summer the frozen pond
at the summit was loud with mating frogs.
Woodpeckers beat a tattoo on trunks
and squirrels were busy.

Nothing moves now but clouds
and their shadows on the snow and ours
and the *cumuli humils* of our breath
leading us on.

# On the Bridge at Treman Gorge

*for Zellman*

We stand on the bridge watching the water.
Leaves land on the surface, turn
this way and that, distracted from the flow

into eddies, changing direction, the smallest
joining a swirl of bubbles in a vortex.
I see it as a pattern that pleases the eye.

You see it obeying Lagrange's equations.
In nature, you've taught me, nothing
is truly random; the laminar flow

devolves into turbulence, order into disorder
without apparent pattern and yet a child
makes order of a cloud, scalloping

its edges into arched puffs, and water
in its wildest flow braids itself
like a woman's hair. The almost infinite

degrees of freedom in turbulent motion
should end in chaos but order creeps in,
an order the eye finds in disorder.

## The Lost Map

It lay beside the trail where I dropped it
three weeks ago on Christmas Day.
Ice had made the trail treacherous
and you slipped, one foot hanging
above the gorge where water curdled
at the edge of its flow. Fear made me careless
of all save footholds on the glazed snow
as we edged back to the trail-head.

This morning's sun lit patches of snow
like sea-spume flung on the slope
as we re-traced our steps beside the gorge
and there it was beside the path,
the lost map folded to fit my pocket
and I was blithe with delight as if
a living thing had strayed and not a sheet
creased in two, its ink still bright.

I'd marked each section of trail:
a year's progress left to right
across the map, walks for all seasons,
sepia to emerald, flame red to gray,
nesting herons, spring-startled grouse,
scutter of deer, a slow snake;
this time, too, when the woods are all ours,
and a lost map is safe on snow.

## Near Field

Because fog blurs the forest
we focus on the near field,
the copper cuirass of leaves
underfoot that shields

the orange eft and other
small-fry from snow's weight,
ferns green as go,
their long fronds delicate

yet oddly sturdy in the cold.
At the forest's edge we surprise
a ruffed grouse and a couple
kissing. She starts to apologize:

*Not used to seeing people
around here. Thought
we had it all to ourselves.*
But we were glad we caught

the couple kissing, the bird
startled, thundering upwards,
the near field fog revealed
when it blurred the woods.

## Blowsy

Flowers fall sideways
like drunks for comfort, aging
leaves dab on blush
before they litter the lawn.

Golden-rod grows heavy
and tilts above purple aster;
mauve crocuses collapse
around their tender stems.

There were women once, aging
in flushed disorder, whose hair
came easily undone:
blowsy, they called them.

## Preserves

Each year we picked them—plums
apples, apricots—from crooked trees
that grew around the house, reminders
of a former orchard, beans and peas

picked at nearby farms. Sometimes
my grandfather joined us, slicing fruit
for jam, three generation of hands
at the kitchen table, pickling beetroot,

sterilizing jars, stretching cellophane
dipped in vinegar till heat sucked it in
and a rubber band sealed it tight.
If I could pick this morning like a Crispin

I'd slice it in four—cool shade
climbing the gorge's south rim,
heat on the path down the north side,
diving into the lake for a delicious swim,

and coffee, strong, with an almond croissant
at the café on a creek in the village nearby.
I'd keep it in a jar with a cellophane seal
preserved in syrup for a winter pie.

# III. The Body Forgets

# Naples

In your slanting streets
that fell down worn steps,
washing strung above
like bunting, caged birds
competing with tenor serenades,
whine of motor-scooters,
trams bristling with boys
hanging off the back,
women lifting fish
by their tails to sniff, clams
soon to be *alle vongole*
clattering beside squid and eel,
crabs scrabbling in pails,
I first saw Europe.

The morning fog
still hung in the harbor
turning that slice of life
hemmed between sea and land
into a milky maze
and I walked your streets
enchanted, my lips Dior
scarlet, my life ahead.

## Bangkok Moon

That day we'd seen it on TV
—men bouncing like kids on a trampoline
in its soft inviting dust.

At night we went to a party.
A bowl on the table held grass—
the host handed us pipes.

The moon's new-sullied surface
silvered the Chao Phraya.
Downtown, slim Thai girls

cruised the streets, soldiers
on leave from the war in tow
like children leading buffaloes

to the rice-fields. A smell
of rotten fruit and gasoline
floated in the thick air.

The host took my hand,
and led me, compliant as moon-dust,
to the banks of the river while

the party went on and on
and the moonwalkers slept,
their footprints left behind
like children's on a beach.

## Lisbon Revisited

Along the Tagus the docks are alight
with clubs, discotheques, bars, drugs…
the Euro-glitter of Lisbon by night.
At the tram stop where tiny pastries were sold
the concert-hall blocks the monastery's view;
vast as a stadium it cheats the singer
of her power to charm even those few
who remember her from another life.

Was that the door to the house I lived in?
It doesn't matter now—it's she,
not the Rua de São Bento that's gone,
the girl in green who took the stairs
two at a time with a bag of custard-apples
that April, when the scent of limes
hung in the air like liberation.

I motion the taxi on. Why stop?
There's no return to chapter one,
no chance to write a different plot
and take her backwards out that door,
unbuying her fruit in the fragrant square.
But you, old friend, who stayed behind
(more salt than ginger in your fiery hair)
tell me I seemed strangely unformed

when we met, like the books with uncut pages
sold on barrows in the Avenida da Liberdade,

waiting the slash of a knife at their edges.
I longed to be slit by some canny Pygmalion,
hailed as potential, polished, recast.

And here I am now, a guest of the city—
there must be something to me at last,
a style acquired, a plot that coheres.

# Archaeology

It ploughed furrows of the past
turning up buried sounds
as it circled—dead sopranos,
stride piano players,
forgotten comedians caught
in the narrow plastic grooves
a century after they cut
a side. A cactus needle
would do when we ran out
of metal ones to reveal
Caruso, Galli-Curci, "No,
No, Nanette." Did
spade ever turn up
such brilliant remains of a lost
civilization? What we could hear
through the scratches was a faint copy
of sounds that had thrilled an audience.
No potsherd could tell us
what the spinning disk unearthed
when we turned a handle.
The voices of another age
reached us cracked yet still alive.

# Guardians

We're guardians of each other's memories…
your family quarrels loud enough
to scare neighbors a block away,
your Scottish housekeeper killed crossing
the road to post a letter, are as much
my memories as yours. You remember me
before we met on a horse's back
watching clouds, my father singing
his Music Hall songs. We've grown like
that double tree we saw in the woods:
two trunks, branches inseparable.

But on a hot afternoon in Florida, fan
lazing overhead, you surprise me.
*You've always liked those slow-revolving
Chinese fans*, you say. *What fans?*
I ask. What else do you remember for me?
*You carried a knife before you met me.*
I only know the one I open letters with.

Whose memories are they now?
They grow towards each other until
I'm left with your Scottish housekeeper;
you have my slow fans and a lost knife.

# The Body Forgets

*Θυμίσου σώμα — Remember, Body (Constantine Cavafy)*

The mind forgets. We worry about a name
not retrieved in time or why we went
into a room but the body's guilty too.
The smell of Dior lipstick used to transport me

straight to the Cairo Museum, its dusty shelves
crowded with poorly-sorted relics and a hand
that touched mine and whispered "Eight o'clock,
D-deck." Decades later one sniff was enough.

Now, in the cosmetics department I lift
a lipstick to my nose and nothing happens.
My mind remembers, my body fails to contract
as it did for so long, triggering a spasm

of pure desire. I don't want his name.
It can sink into the Suez Canal with the ship
where my parents drank cocktails and he
waited on the dark deck and kissed

the scarlet from my lips. Now I'm left
with the brand of a lipstick I bought that day;
the body's forgotten what it felt like,
that rush of blood through the veins.

## Pruning

Like vines, the synapses need pruning
or they grow rank and fail to bloom.
Untrimmed connections run riot
and a tangle of branches spells doom,
causing the brain to become bipolar.
Unable to find a single path
it deviates upward, left and right,
its wayward shoots inhibiting growth.

Does memory too need pruning?
Better to forget that neighbor's name
or the film you saw with you know who.
Loss of recall's a winning game
as the mind discards what's overgrown,
lopping off all that's unimportant
to a single stem that may look dead
but to the vintner is a wise relinquishment.

# IV. Three Poems for Jon Stallworthy
(1/18/1935-11/19/2014)

## A Poet's Letters

His letters came stamped with the monarch's head,
his writing, black and handsome as he,
listed eastward on fat envelopes
stuffed with poems, mine and his.

On my poems were only faint marks,
in pencil, ever-so-gentle suggestions,
even praise that rang to my ears
a little disingenuous

but left a warmth behind like sun
on a stone seat. Family news
and literary gossip—Isiah, Akhmatova,
tea with Mrs. Yeats, Owen—

the small talk of great voices
he mined for his poetic purposes.

# Blenheim

In Blenheim Park they re-enact
the Civil War. Even children wear
long skirts, breeches, bonnets;
men's beards are grown all year
to reach a grey, authentic length.
*Get your black powder here!*
says a sign and muskets send
puffs of smoke into the blue May air.

Do they swarm like this across Flanders
fields, where poets raised on a dream
of glory grew cold in a day of war?

How long does it take for a war to seem
a game to re-play on green fields
at Agincourt, Gettysburg, here at Blenheim?

# Re-enactment

My birthday and soon the Great War's.
Beside the guest bed a scarlet rose,
the kind your wife admired—single,
fragrant, and your book of war poems.

You missed the birthday dinner—a problem
you'd had with swallowing but
we could make an early start,
re-trace last year's sunlit walk

through the park to Woodstock and 'The Feathers'.
At breakfast you read a poem you'd chosen
for the book: Hecht's "More Light!
More Light!" *Much casual death*

*had drained away their souls...*then
we paid homage to her garden, flowers
true to their species: wallflower, stock,
a rose she hoped she'd live to see.

No re-enactors disturbed the grass
at Blenheim but you talked of
the war poet you were and the love poet
you wished you'd been, watched swans

glide above their darker doubles.
You spoke of a woman you loved who
flew, decades ago, to spend

two nights with you at the end of Africa,

now alone. You wondered where
this might lead as we found a table—the same
as last year. We drank wine
and laughed, ignorant of the dark mass

couched in your throat, the strangler
about to close its grip. We spoke
of next year's re-enactment as if
an endless succession of sunlit walks

stretched ahead; a kiss at the station
to seal our promise, I left for home.
A week later came a call, the verdict
of your test. Your warm voice chilled me:

"Chance of parole small."
Barely a year since your wife's funeral,
then came Seamus' turn. No death
is casual for lovers or friends. And you,

a war poet, were always a poet
of love—no death drained the soul
from you as you battled to name,
remember, pity the ones death chose.

Here, in a still bright autumn,
no news from the Front. I try to read
silence as hope. Next year, I say,

we'll re-enact our walk, our talk.

ii

*I am the woman who went to Africa...*
she wrote, knowing all I knew
of her was this, that she came to him
because he called and asked her to.

A lifetime later, unasked, she came
to share what time was left. No sooner
had he found his youthful muse
than life was forfeit to his cancer.

As she sat there beside his bed
there were moments, surely, together again,
when suddenly the autumn garden glittered
beyond a window, bright with rain,

and eye met eye, hand sought hand,
and they forgot the future, wordless
in the presence of an unexpected rapture
that lit the hours before the darkness.

# Acknowledgements

"Afghanistan, 1969" was published in *BookPress*.
"A Stray Metaphor" and "Drawer by Drawer"
were published in *Antipodes*.
"Garden Wars" was published in *Seneca Review*.
"A Willing Heart" was published in *Forward*.
"Blowsy" was published in *Per Contra*.
"Flood Days" was set to music by Kate Whitely
and presented at the concert "Water-culture:
Women's Work(s)", Oxford, in 2013.

Thanks to my dear friends in poetry who read
and commented on these poems, especially
Chana Kronfeld, David Curzon, Philip Ramp,
Greg Delanty, John Lucas and the Aladdin's poets
(Laura Glenn, Peter Fortunato & Jack Hopper).
Thanks to my lifelong friend, Michael Rubbo, for
permission to use his rubbing "By the Seine" as a
cover illustration.

A warm thanks to editors Marc Estrin and Donna
Bister of Fomite, who continue to publish books
they believe in.

Fomite

**About Fomite**

*A fomite is a medium capable of transmitting infectious organisms from one individual to another.*

"The activity of art is based on the capacity of people to be infected by the feelings of others." Tolstoy, *What Is Art?*

Writing a review on Amazon, Good Reads, Shelfari, Library Thing or other social media sites for readers will help the progress of independent publishing. To submit a review, go to the book page on any of the sites and follow the links for reviews. Books from independent presses rely on reader to reader communications.

For more information or to order any of our books, visit
http://www.fomitepress.com/FOMITE/Our_Books.html

**More Titles from Fomite...**

**Novels**
Joshua Amses— *Ghatsr*
Joshua Amses— *During This, Our Nadir*
Joshua Amses— *Raven or Crow*
Joshua Amses— *The Moment Before an Injury*
Jaysinh Birjepatel— *The Good Muslim of Jackson Heights*
Jaysinh Birjepatel— *Nothing Beside Remains*
David Brizer— *Victor Rand*
Paula Closson Buck— *Summer on the Cold War Planet*
Dan Chodorkoff— *Loisaida*
David Adams Cleveland— *Time's Betrayal*

Fomite

Jaimee Wriston Colbert— *Vanishing Acts*
Roger Coleman— *Skywreck Afternoons*
Marc Estrin— *Hyde*
Marc Estrin— *Kafka's Roach*
Marc Estrin— *Speckled Vanities*
Zdravka Evtimova— *In the Town of Joy and Peace*
Zdravka Evtimova— *Sinfonia Bulgarica*
Daniel Forbes — *Derail This Train Wreck*
Greg Guma— *Dons of Time*
Richard Hawley— *The Three Lives of Jonathan Force*
Lamar Herrin— *Father Figure*
Michael Horner— *Damage Control*
Ron Jacobs— *All the Sinners Saints*
Ron Jacobs— *Short Order Frame Up*
Ron Jacobs— *The Co-conspirator's Tale*
Scott Archer Jones— *And Throw the Skins Away*
Scott Archer Jones— *A Rising Tide of People Swept Away*
Julie Justicz— *A Boy Called Home*
Maggie Kast— *A Free Unsullied Land*
Darrell Kastin— *Shadowboxing with Bukowski*
Coleen Kearon— *Feminist on Fire*
Coleen Kearon— *#triggerwarning*
Jan Englis Leary— *Thicker Than Blood*
Diane Lefer— *Confessions of a Carnivore*
Rob Lenihan— *Born Speaking Lies*
Colin Mitchell— *Roadman*
Ilan Mochari— *Zinsky the Obscure*
Peter Nash— *Parsimony*
Peter Nash— *The Perfection of Things*
Gregory Papadoyiannis— *The Baby Jazz*

Fomite

Pelham — *The Walking Poor*
Andy Potok — *My Father's Keeper*
Kathryn Roberts — *Companion Plants*
Robert Rosenberg — *Isles of the Blind*
Fred Russell — *Rafi's World*
Ron Savage — *Voyeur in Tangier*
David Schein — *The Adoption*
Lynn Sloan — *Principles of Navigation*
L.E. Smith — *The Consequence of Gesture*
L.E. Smith — *Travers' Inferno*
L.E. Smith — *Untimely RIPped*
Bob Sommer — *A Great Fullness*
Tom Walker — *A Day in the Life*
Susan V. Weiss — *My God, What Have We Done?*
Peter M. Wheelwright — *As It Is On Earth*
Suzie Wizowaty — *The Return of Jason Green*

**Poetry**

Anna Blackmer — *Hexagrams*
Antonello Borra — *Alfabestiario*
Antonello Borra — *AlphaBetaBestiaro*
Sue D. Burton — *Little Steel*
David Cavanagh — *Cycling in Plato's Cave*
James Connolly — *Picking Up the Bodies*
Greg Delanty — *Loosestrife*
Mason Drukman — *Drawing on Life*
J. C. Ellefson — *Foreign Tales of Exemplum and Woe*
Tina Escaja/Mark Eisner — *Caida Libre/Free Fall*
Anna Faktorovich — *Improvisational Arguments*
Barry Goldensohn — *Snake in the Spine, Wolf in the Heart*

Fomite

Barry Goldensohn— *The Hundred Yard Dash Man*
Barry Goldensohn— *The Listener Aspires to the Condition of Music*
R. L. Green — *When You Remember Deir Yassin*
Gail Holst-Warhaft— *Lucky Country*
Raymond Luczak— *A Babble of Objects*
Kate Magill— *Roadworthy Creature, Roadworthy Craft*
Tony Magistrale— *Entanglements*
Andreas Nolte— *Mascha: The Poems of Mascha Kaléko*
Sherry Olson— *Four-Way Stop*
David Polk— *Drinking the River*
Aristea Papalexandrou/Philip Ramp— *Μας προσπερνά/It's Passing Us By*
Janice Miller Potter— *Meanwell*
Philip Ramp— *The Melancholy of a Life as the Joy of Living It Slowly Chills*
Joseph D. Reich— *Connecting the Dots to Shangrila*
Joseph D. Reich— *The Hole That Runs Through Utopia*
Joseph D. Reich— *The Housing Market*
Joseph D. Reich— *The Derivation of Cowboys and Indians*
Kennet Rosen and Richard Wilson— *Gomorrah*
Fred Rosenblum— *Vietnumb*
David Schein— *My Murder and Other Local News*
Harold Schweizer— *Miriam's Book*
Scott T. Starbuck— *Industrial Oz*
Scott T. Starbuck— *Hawk on Wire*
Scott T. Starbuck— *Carbonfish Blues*
Seth Steinz or— *Among the Lost*
Seth Steinzor— *To Join the Lost*
Susan Thomas— *The Empty Notebook Interrogates Itself*
Susan Thomas— *In the Sadness Museum*
Paolo Valesio/Todd Portnowitz— *La Mezzanotte di Spoleto/Midnight in Spoleto*

Fomite

Sharon Webster— *Everyone Lives Here*
Tony Whedon— *The Tres Riches Heures*
Tony Whedon— *The Falkland Quartet*
Claire Zoghb— *Dispatches from Everest*

**Stories**
Jay Boyer— *Flight*
Michael Cocchiarale— *Still Time*
Michael Cocchiarale— *Here Is Ware*
Neil Connelly— *In the Wake of Our Vows*
Catherine Zobal Dent— *Unfinished Stories of Girls*
Zdravka Evtimova —*Carts and Other Stories*
John Michael Flynn — *Off to the Next Wherever*
Derek Furr— *Semitones*
Derek Furr— *Suite for Three Voices*
Elizabeth Genovise— *Where There Are Two or More*
Andrei Guriuanu— *Body of Work*
Zeke Jarvis— *In A Family Way*
Arya Jenkins— *Blue Songs in an Open Key*
Jan Englis Leary— *Skating on the Vertical*
Marjorie Maddox— *What She Was Saying*
William Marquess— *Boom-shacka-lacka*
Gary Miller— *Museum of the Americas*
Jennifer Anne Moses— *Visiting Hours*
Martin Ott— *Interrogations*
Jack Pulaski— *Love's Labours*
Charles Rafferty— *Saturday Night at Magellan's*
Ron Savage— *What We Do For Love*
Fred Skolnik— *Americans and Other Stories*
Lynn Sloan— *This Far Is Not Far Enough*

Fomite

L.E. Smith— *Views Cost Extra*
Caitlin Hamilton Summie— *To Lay To Rest Our Ghosts*
Susan Thomas— *Among Angelic Orders*
Tom Walker— *Signed Confessions*
Silas Dent Zobal— *The Inconvenience of the Wings*

**Odd Birds**
Micheal Breiner— *the way none of this happened*
J. C. Ellefson — *Under the Influence*
David Ross Gunn— *Cautionary Chronicles*
Andrei Guriuanu and Teknari— *The Darkest City*
Gail Holst-Warhaft— *The Fall of Athens*
Roger Leboitz— *A Guide to the Western Slopes and the Outlying Area*
dug Nap— *Artsy Fartsy*
Delia Bell Robinson— *A Shirtwaist Story*
Peter Schumann— *Bread & Sentences*
Peter Schumann— *Charlotte Salomon*
Peter Schumann— *Faust 3*
Peter Schumann— *Planet Kasper, Volumes One and Two*
Peter Schumann— *We*

**Plays**
Stephen Goldberg— *Screwed and Other Plays*
Michele Markarian— *Unborn Children of America*

**Essays**
William Benton— *Eye Contact*
Robert Sommer— *Losing Francis*

www.ingramcontent.com/pod-product-compliance
Lightning Source LLC
Chambersburg PA
CBHW020130130526
44591CB00032B/586